PLANET
SOS
SPACE
CHALLENGE

Gerry Bailey

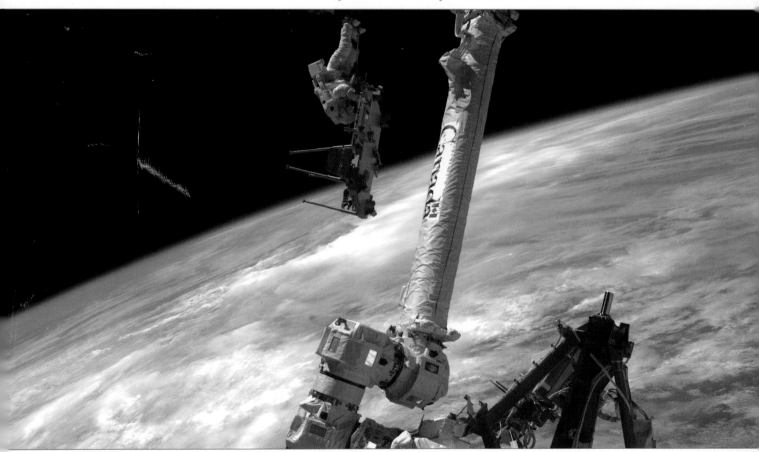

Gareth Stevens
Publishing

Please visit our Web site, www.garethstevens.com. For a free color catalog of all our high-quality books, call toll free 1-800-542-2595 or fax 1-877-542-2596.

Library of Congress Cataloging-in-Publication Data

Bailey, Gerry.
  Space challenge / Gerry Bailey.
      p. cm. — (Planet SOS)
  Includes index.
  ISBN 978-1-4339-4982-1 (library binding)
  ISBN 978-1-4339-4983-8 (pbk.)
  ISBN 978-1-4339-4984-5 (6-pack)
  1. Astronautics—Juvenile literature. 2. Outer space—Exploration—Juvenile literature. I. Title.
  TL793.B224 2011
  629.4—dc22
                                              2010032884

Published in 2011 by
Gareth Stevens Publishing
111 East 14th Street, Suite 349
New York, NY 10003

Designer: Simon Webb
Editor: Felicia Law

Printed in the United States of America

CPSIA compliance information: Batch #CW11GS: For further information contact Gareth Stevens, New York, New York at 1-800-542-2595.

CONTENTS

OUR UNIVERSE   4–5
ORBITING OBJECTS   6–15
ENERGY MAKER   16–25
OUT OF THE SKY   26–29
PROBING MARS   30–31
TELESCOPES   32–35
COMETS   36–37
VACATION IN SPACE   38–39
LUNAR LANDING   40–41
HELPING HAND   42–43
GLOSSARY   44–45
INDEX   46–47

OUR UNIVERSE

We live on a planet that orbits the sun in a solar system. It's the third planet from the sun. Our sun is located in one arm of a spiral galaxy, and the galaxy is made up of billions of suns, called stars. It swirls around in space with other galaxies. We call this massive amount of space our universe. And it's getting bigger all the time.

A start

Our universe hasn't always been here. Scientists think it came into being about 15 billion years ago. Before that, everything that created the universe was packed so tightly that it made just a tiny point, smaller than an atom, called a singularity.

As well as being tiny, the singularity was very hot, perhaps billions and billions of degrees. Then, something amazing happened. The singularity exploded. Scientists call it the Big Bang although it almost certainly wasn't that kind of big explosion. Everything was thrown outwards and our universe began. The Big Bang was so powerful that material is still moving away today.

About 300,000 years after the Big Bang, the temperature had dropped low enough for atoms to form. Expanding gas clouds soon filled the universe and after millions of years, early galaxies began to form. After a billion years the first spiral galaxies with stars appeared.

Thousands of sparkling young stars make up the giant nebula NGC 3603, one of the largest star clusters in the Milky Way.

Measuring space

Astronomers measure the huge distances of space in light-years. A light-year is the distance light travels in one year, at a speed of 186,411 miles (300,000 km) per second. That's around 5.9 trillion miles (9.5 trillion km).

ORBITING OBJECTS

Before the invention of rockets, humans looked at space through telescopes of various kinds. Today, rockets can launch telescopes into space on probes and satellites. Probes send back data about the planets and other objects they approach. Satellites orbit Earth collecting and sending data. Space telescopes can send back pictures that are much clearer than any earthbound telescope.

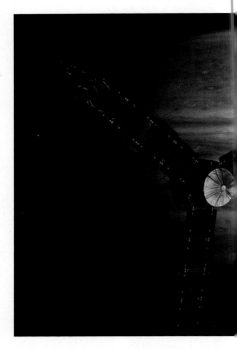

The satellite Juno will travel to Jupiter. It will measure its huge magnetic field and the amount of water and ammonia in the planet's thick cloud cover, as well as carrying out other tasks.

Orbits

Orbits are said to be either closed (moving around something) or open (moving in a curve that never joins up). Man-made satellites take both orbits. A satellite positioned 22,238 miles (35,790 km) above the equator takes 24 hours to orbit the Earth, making it seem to hover over one spot. This is called a "geosynchronous" orbit. Weather and communications satellites take this kind of orbit.

The lower an orbit is, the faster the satellite has to go to resist the pull of Earth's gravity. A low Earth orbit is around 186 miles (300 km) above Earth's surface. Compare this to a jet plane that flies only 7 miles (12 km) above the ground.

An orbit that passes over the North and South Poles is called a polar orbit. It allows the satellite to survey the whole planet as it spins below.

Sun

Mercury

Venus

Earth

Mars

Jupiter

asteroid belt

Saturn

Uranus

Neptune

The planets of the solar system orbit the sun on elliptical (oval-shaped) paths. Mercury, closest to the sun, has the shortest orbit. Beyond Neptune are other objects in orbit, including Pluto.

The planet Saturn has rings made from water ice mixed with dust and chemicals that orbit it constantly.

Man-made satellites

As well as one natural satellite, Earth has around 25,000 man-made ones that are constantly orbiting it. The first satellite launched into space was called Sputnik 1. It was launched by the Soviet Union October 4, 1957. It was a ball of metal just 23 inches (58 cm) in diameter. After transmitting temperature information for 22 days it ran out of energy and burned up in the atmosphere.

Since then many satellites have been sent into space to do a variety of jobs. They are used to study the universe, help forecast the weather, transfer telephone calls, help ships and aircraft to navigate, and for spying.

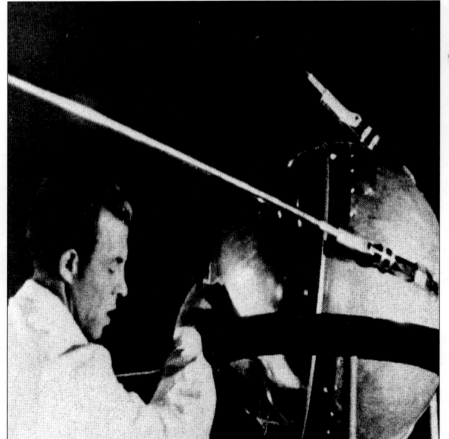

Meteosat was an early weather satellite that provided images of Earth and its cloud cover every 30 minutes.

Sputnik 1 was the first satellite launched into space.

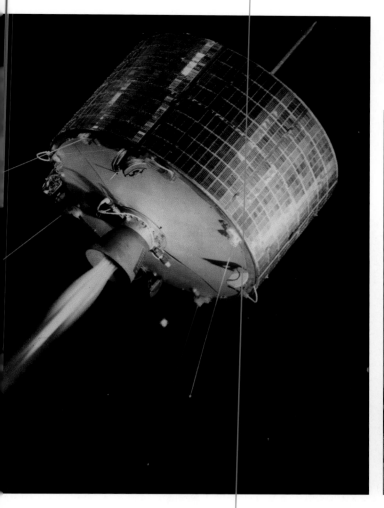

The first Syncom communication satellites went into orbit at a speed that matched Earth's own orbit.

GOES-11 is an American satellite that collects information to help with weather forecasting.

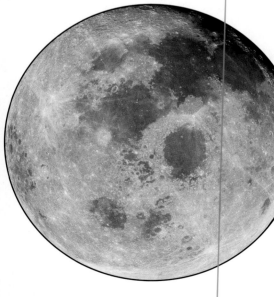

The moon is Earth's one natural satellite.

Natural satellites

A satellite is an object that orbits, or travels around another object, such as a planet, in space. The moon is our natural satellite, which means that it isn't man-made. It orbits Earth every 27 Earth days, 7 hours, 43 minutes and 11.5 seconds. The moon maintains its orbit because of its own gravity and Earth's gravity.

Shuttles have a payload area in which they carry objects such as telescopes into orbit.

The space shuttle is made up of the craft itself and its external rocket launchers.

Space shuttle

The first rockets used for the orbital space exploration could be used only once. NASA wanted something that could be used again and again, and developed the space shuttle. A space shuttle is launched with rockets but lands like an aircraft on a runway. The first space shuttle flight was made by the shuttle *Columbia* April 12, 1981.

Payload

Space shuttles are designed with a payload (cargo) bay so that they can transport equipment into space. They are used to take astronauts to space stations, to do maintenance work on satellites or to transport items such as the Hubble Space Telescope into orbit. The space shuttle is now delivering equipment to the International Space Station.

Dangerous flight

Most shuttle flights take off and land safely. But it takes a lot of effort by many scientists and technicians to make this happen. Sometimes, though, things go wrong, such as in January 1986 when the ill-fated *Challenger* shuttle exploded on takeoff. Then, in February 2003, just 16 minutes before scheduled touchdown, *Columbia* was destroyed. Both accidents set back the shuttle program, but didn't end it.

International Space Station

The International Space Station is a research facility that operates in space. Construction began back in 1998 and it is still being assembled. It is being developed by a team of five international space agencies and will continue to orbit Earth at a low level for the next ten years or so.

The first section was the Russian-built Zarya control module that was launched in November 1998. The first crew arrived two years later, and it was another year before the space station was continuously occupied, becoming home to three long-term residents at a time. Each mission lasts around six months.

A growing project

A total of around 70 flights of Russian Proton rockets and American space shuttles will be needed to complete the space station. Currently, the space station is made up of 13 pressurized modules and a connecting truss structure. It is powered by sunlight, using 16 solar arrays mounted on the outer truss framework.

Nearly 80 different crew have so far lived on board. They have come from many different countries and are both men and women. Up to five or six astronauts live there at any one time.

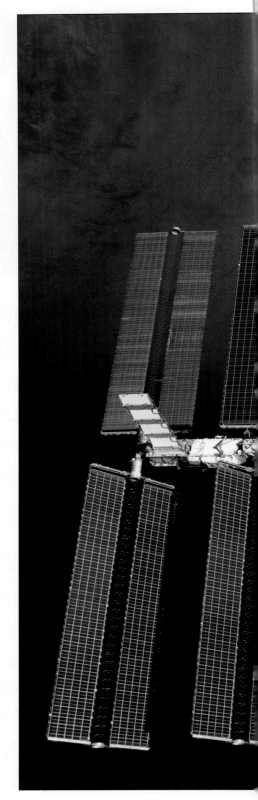

Astronauts must get used to cramped conditions.

Debris in space

When a Russian and an American satellite collided over Siberia it was considered a very unusual event. But some scientists don't think it was so unusual. They believe the chances of a collision in space are getting larger. And that's partly because space is becoming littered with man-made debris.

Surveillance

There are so many objects orbiting in space that the United States set up the US Space Surveillance Network. This can track space objects as small as 4 inches (10 cm) in diameter. The European Space Agency has now set up a similar system. Most of the objects they track are known as "space junk" – useless pieces of man-made debris.

Space junk

Bits of space junk may be small, but they can damage working spacecraft. Much of it comes from space missions that leave odd pieces of stuff around such as rocket stages, satellite pieces, nuts and bolts, rubbish bags and even paint chips. These pieces of junk travel at average speeds of 22,369 miles (36,000 km) per hour. So if they hit something, it could be catastrophic. A metal sphere the size of a tennis ball, for example, would have the same effect as 25 sticks of dynamite. Out of the estimated 600,000 objects more than 0.4 inches (1 cm) in diameter, only 19,000 can be tracked as of today.

Burned-out rocket boosters and fuel tanks are also space junk.

Avoiding a collision

Space shuttles have sometimes had to alter their flight path to avoid debris. Some scientists think it's time to start removing some of the junk.

British scientists are experimenting with a device to drag space junk out of orbit. The CubeSail is a tiny satellite cube that uses a 270-sq-foot (25-sq-m) plastic sheet. Attached to larger satellites or space debris, the sail would catch air molecules still present in low Earth orbit and pull the object out of its orbit to burn up in the atmosphere.

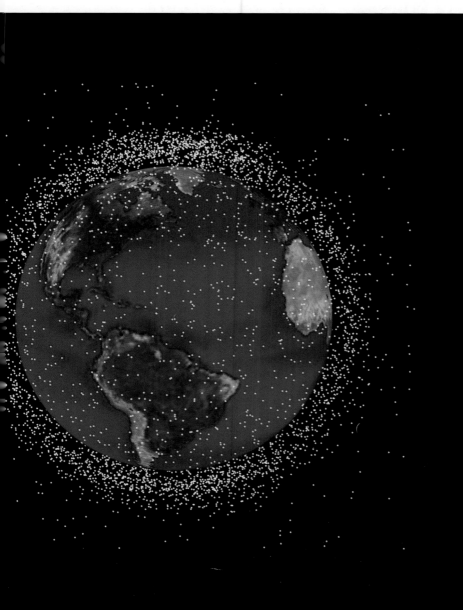

This shows the distribution of space junk that's at least 4 inches (10 cm) in diameter and in low Earth orbit.

15

ENERGY MAKER

Our sun is the closest star to Earth. Scientists believe it was formed around 5 billion years ago. The sun is vital to us because it is our most important source of energy. The tremendous heat inside the sun causes particles of hydrogen gas to hit each other and join up, forming helium. They give off energy as they do this, and it finds its way to the photosphere, or surface of the sun, escaping as light and heat.

Solar activity

Along with creating light and heat there are other activities that take place on the sun's surface. These include sunspots, solar flares, and solar prominences. Sunspots happen when the sun's magnetic field reaches the surface and cools it down, making the area darker.

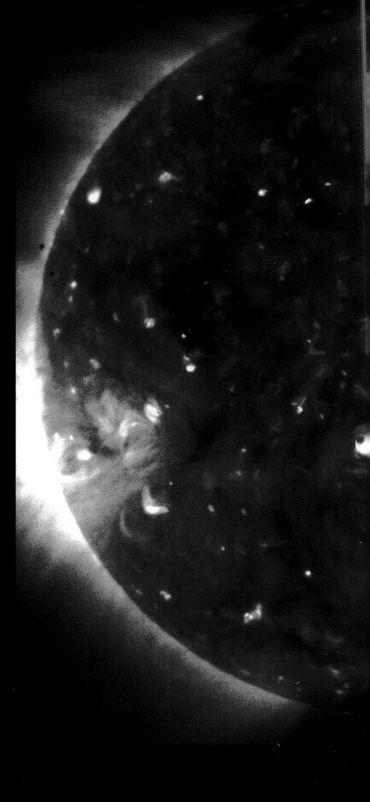

The northern lights, or aurora borealis, are caused by the solar wind hitting our atmosphere where the magnetic field dips to the North Pole.

Space weather

The sun throws out around a million tons of material into space each second. This creates the solar wind that makes up space weather. This wind is even more gusty when a solar flare erupts, sending more particles and radiation into space. The particles include protons, alpha particles and electrons. Radiation includes gamma rays and X rays. Earth's magnetic field protects us from the harmful radiation, but astronauts have to take extra care. They don't, for example, go out on space walks after a solar flare has erupted.

The magnetic fields produce clouds of glowing gas above the photosphere called prominences. Most brilliant, though, are solar flares. These are bursts of energy that throw out streams of particles as well as X rays and radio waves from the sun.

Sunspots follow an 11-year cycle between maximum periods of activity. They can affect the power output of the sun, and might have an effect on the global warming of Earth.

Disappearing Sun

Every so often a shadow passes across the sun, and Earth is plunged into darkness. When the moon's orbit takes it between Earth and the sun, it can block out the sun. This is called an eclipse of the sun. This doesn't happen very often, as the plane of the moon's orbit is at an angle to that of Earth, so they hardly ever line up exactly.

Total eclipse

Even though there are great differences in their size, the sun and moon appear to be about the same diameter in the sky. That's because they are such a huge distance from Earth. When they line up exactly, the shadow cast by the moon covers Earth and there is a total eclipse. The sky goes as dark as night and you can see the stars. The shadow that causes a total eclipse is the umbra. Around it is a lighter shadow called the penumbra. If you're in the area covered by the penumbra you see only a partial eclipse, as only part of the sun will be covered. The umbra can be up to 158 miles (255 km) across.

The phases of a solar eclipse.

The sun's corona is revealed when the sun is fully eclipsed by the moon.

When light from the sun is blocked by the moon it creates a total shadow called an umbra and a partial one around it called a penumbra.

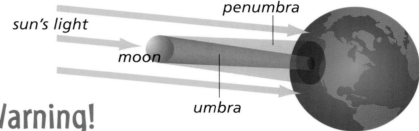

sun's light
penumbra
moon
umbra

Warning!

You must never attempt to view a solar eclipse by looking at the sun, or by using a telescope or binoculars. The sun's rays can cause permanent damage to your eyesight, or blindness. Do not use ordinary light filters, such as sunglasses, because they will not filter out the sun's harmful rays.

Astronomers watch an eclipse.

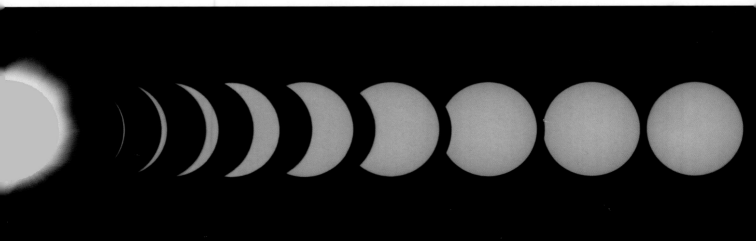

Radiation peril

Almost all the energy that drives life and growth on Earth comes from the sun. Solar energy radiates down to us in different kinds of waves, the most powerful of which is ultraviolet (UV) radiation. While some radiation is healthy, high levels can weaken our immune system and make us less resistant to infection and disease and more prone to developing cancers.

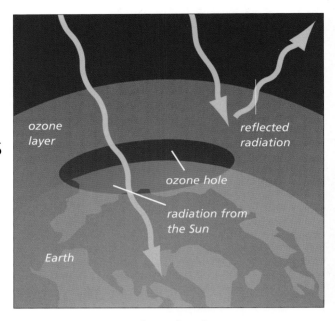

What protects Earth from UV rays is a layer of ozone that's located up in the second layer of our atmosphere. Ozone is a particular kind of oxygen gas that has the ability to absorb ultraviolet radiation.

Disappearing ozone

But there's a problem. There's a big hole in the ozone layer, so more and more dangerous UV radiation has been reaching us on Earth. It started about 50 years ago and was mainly caused by pollution on Earth and by CFCs in particular.

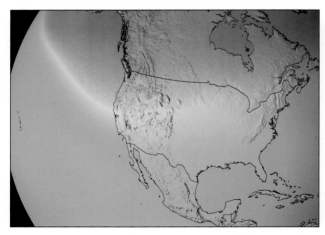

The red to yellow area shows the higher concentration of ozone cover in 1966.

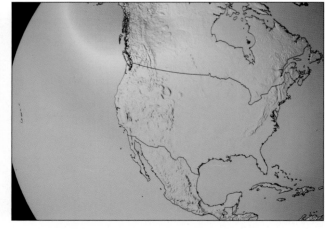

By 2002 the cover was reduced.

CFCs

CFC stands for chlorofluorocarbon. CFCs have been used in aerosols, in refrigerators and in the electronics industry. And they stay in the atmosphere for a long time, finally drifting up into the stratosphere and destroying ozone.

After scientists discovered holes in the ozone layer, CFCs were eventually phased out. The ozone layer is repairing itself, but it will take until about 2050, or longer, before the process is complete.

Aerosols produced CFCs that can destroy our precious ozone layer.

The projected cover by 2020 if CFCs had not been phased out.

A dangerous place

Space is a dangerous place for humans not only because it has no oxygen, but also because it contains damaging radiation. This includes radiation from the sun in the form of the solar wind, as well as gamma rays from newborn black holes and cosmic rays from exploding stars. Perhaps the most dangerous threat to astronauts is galactic cosmic rays, or GCRs. These are particles caused by supernova explosions, traveling at almost the speed of light. They can penetrate the shell of a spaceship and damage human cells.

Death of a star

When a star larger than our sun finally dies, it goes out with a bang. It's called a supernova explosion. Astronomers can see the remains of supernova explosions as glowing gas and dust. The explosion sends the outer layer of the star into space, but the inner core collapses in on itself, pulled by its own gravity. The result is a tiny neutron star.

Neutron stars

A neutron star has a radius of around 6 to 9 miles (10 to 15 km). But it has a greater mass than our sun, which is 621,371 miles (1 million km) across. Mass describes the amount of material in an object. So all the stuff in a neutron star has to be packed tightly together.

Pulsars

Neutron stars give off pulses of radiation, including radio waves and light waves. They are called pulsars. As the star gets smaller it spins faster on its axis. At the same time its magnetic field gets stronger and beams of radiation are sent out through the star's magnetic poles.

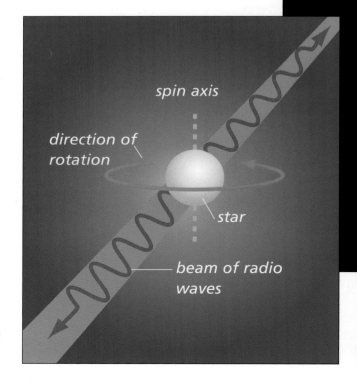

spin axis

direction of rotation

star

beam of radio waves

This diagram shows the spin axis and the magnetic axis of a pulsar.

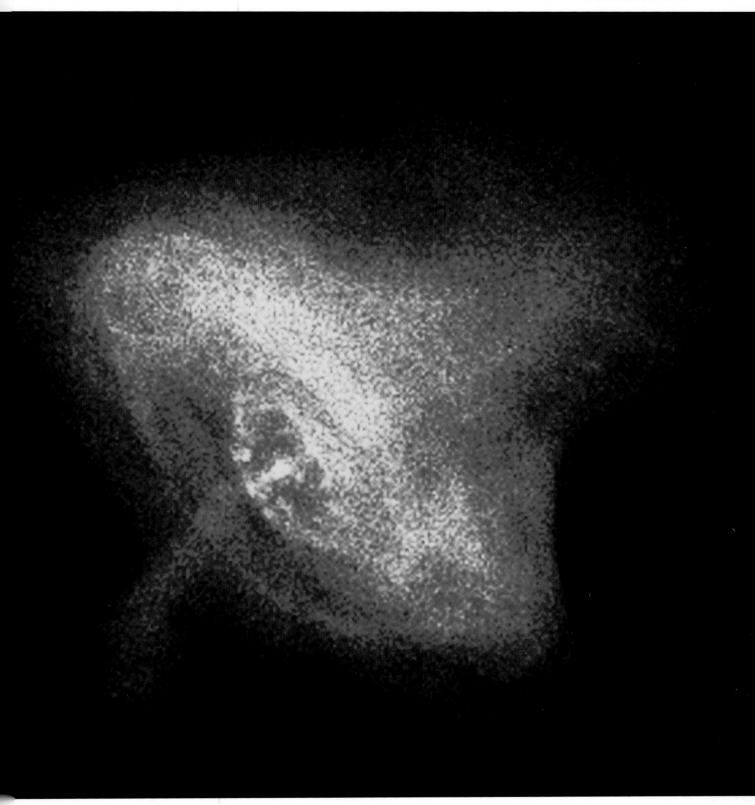

On Earth one teaspoonful of neutron star would weigh 1.1 billion tons (1 billion metric tons). It can have a magnetic field a million times stronger than the strongest ones found on Earth.

Solar sails

Rocket motors are used to propel most spacecraft in space. They need a lot of fuel, in either liquid form or solid form, so they're big and heavy. Now scientists have developed a new kind of propulsion for use in space that uses sunlight. It's called a solar sail.

Pushed by light

Usually we don't feel the force or pressure of sunlight. It is so weak compared to other things in our environment, such as winds or gravity, that we don't notice it. But in space, where there is no atmosphere and much less pull from gravity, the movement of light can be harnessed and used to push objects.

Solar sails don't work like wind sails on Earth. Instead they're very large mirrors that reflect sunlight. As the photons, or particles of light energy, strike the sail they bounce off. This transfers momentum to the sail and pushes it along.

Constant acceleration

Because the photons are constantly hitting the sail and because there are so many of them there is a continual pressure, or push. This constantly accelerates the spacecraft to which the sail is attached. Over time it builds up speed even greater than that produced by a rocket engine.

A solar sail design with the space shuttle in the distance.

Durable

Solar sails have to be durable to withstand the charged particles and micrometeoroids it might encounter in space. They must be lightweight and have a large area to catch as many particles as possible so as to create more power.

OUT OF THE SKY

Space is filled with particles of dust, rock and grit called meteoroids. Most of the dust is from the tails of comets. Each day around 1,100 tons (1,000 metric tons) of stuff from space falls on Earth. Most of these particles are so small, they are slowed down by friction as they hit our atmosphere and gently float to the ground. They are called micrometeorites.

Shooting stars

Larger particles, usually about the size of a pea, burn up in a flash of light. They are called meteors or, sometimes, shooting stars.

When a piece of debris gets as far as Earth's surface it's called a meteorite. Meteorites leave trails of light and can sometimes look like balls of fire. Some meteorites are small pieces of asteroids that have crossed Earth's orbit around the sun. They can also be chunks of other planets.

Meteor showers are named after the constellation where they seem to appear.

Meteor showers

As a comet orbits the sun its dust tail spreads out into a band much wider than the tail itself. When the Earth passes through one of these bands, many of the dust particles enter its atmosphere. The result is called a meteor shower. The particles look as if they are all coming from one direction, but that's a trick of perspective.

Barringer Crater, also called Meteor Crater, is a gigantic hole in the Arizona desert 0.7 miles (1.2 km) across and 574 feet (175 m) deep. It was formed about 50,000 years ago by the impact of a huge meteorite.

Asteroids

At one time some astronomers thought there must be a planet lying between the orbits of Mars and Jupiter. What they found were thousands of tiny objects that came to be known as asteroids. They are also called minor planets.

At first it was believed that they were the result of a planet that had exploded. But now scientists agree that they exist because when the solar system began there was not enough material among them to create one big planet. They were also influenced by the gravity of Jupiter.

The Dawn spacecraft has been sent to investigate Vesta and Ceres. These are two planet-like masses that orbit in the main asteroid belt of the solar system.

Large and small

The largest asteroid is called Ceres. It's about 620 miles (1,000 km) across. Pallas and Vesta are around 310 miles (500 km) across. The smallest ones are just a few miles across, and there are many asteroids of different sizes in between.

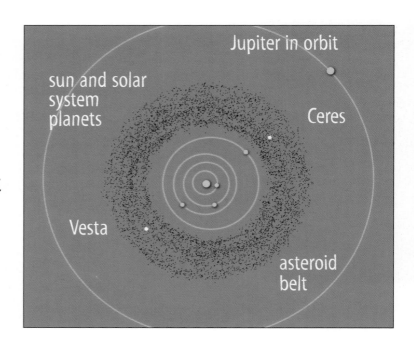

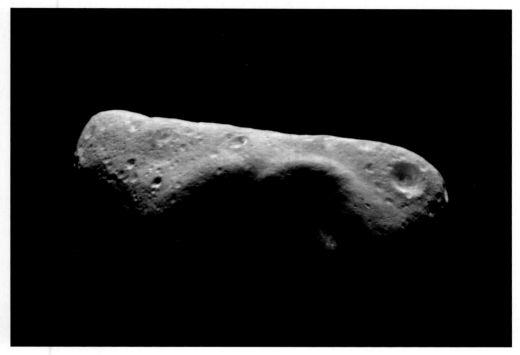

This is the asteroid Eros. The NEAR Shoemaker probe was sent to explore asteroids and sent back this photo.

The asteroid Gaspra is about 12 miles (19 km) across. You can see the craters on its surface caused by collisions with other asteroids

Trojans and near-Earth objects

Not all asteroids exist in the main asteroid belt. Some asteroids have been captured by the gravitational pull of Jupiter. Called trojans, they can be found either ahead of the planet or behind it along its orbit. Other asteroids have orbits that bring them close to Earth. They are known as near-Earth asteroids. Some scientists are concerned that one of these might hit Earth one day.

PROBING MARS

Scientists are now turning to the planet Mars as the next space destination. Mars is the fourth planet from the sun and the second closest to Earth. Venus is the closest, but with its surface temperature of 869°F (465°C) and its sulphuric acid clouds, we cannot go there. For many years scientists wondered if there had been or if there still was life on Mars. To find out, space probes were sent from Earth to observe the red planet.

Space probes are unmanned spacecraft designed to orbit or land on faraway worlds. They carry instruments to record and send back information. Probes can be powered by solar energy or nuclear energy.

Viking landing

In 1976 two *Viking* probes landed on Mars. They carried instruments designed to trace even the tiniest microbes. But they found no trace of life. Their photographs showed the soil colored red by the action of water on small amounts of iron.

More recent probes, including *Pathfinder*, *Spirit* and *Opportunity*, involve robot rovers that trundle across the surface of Mars sending back spectacular photographs and analyzing the rocks and soil.

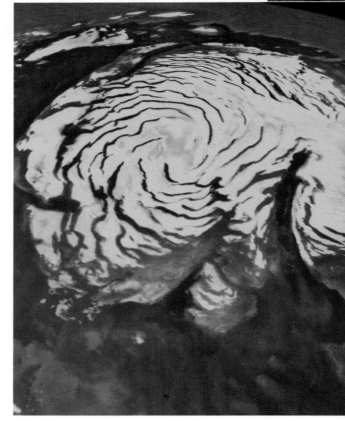

Mars has polar ice caps made of ice surrounded by frozen carbon dioxide, or dry ice.

Rover probes search for clues to Mars's past.

Living on Mars

Scientists believe the remains of dried-up water channels show that water must have existed on the planet many millions of years ago. Mars has a thin atmosphere, but it is made up mostly of carbon dioxide, so it would be no use for humans to breathe. Also the lack of air pressure would turn your blood to steam, so a visitor would have to be well protected.

TELESCOPES

Telescopes allow us to see distant objects more clearly. They can be installed in satellites up in space, where there is no air to affect their view. On Earth, radio telescopes pick up radio waves from space.

Telescopes located all over the world work together to produce more detailed information.

Optical telescopes

Optical telescopes concentrate the light from distant objects, making them appear both larger and brighter. The first ones used lenses to do this, but most of today's large telescopes use huge mirrors instead. To see faint objects, telescopes point at exactly the same spot for minutes or even hours, to collect all the light they can and gradually build up an image. The best telescopes are constructed on mountains in dry areas, where the air is thin and there are few clouds.

The Arecibo Observatory is one of the world's largest radio telescopes, located in Puerto Rico.

An optical telescope in Almeria, southern Spain.

Radio telescopes

Radio telescopes use bowl-shaped dishes to reflect and concentrate radio waves from space to a central point, called an antenna. Computers decode the signals and use this information to produce maps of the sky. In most cases, the dish can be moved in order to pinpoint a particular area of sky.

Radio telescopes in Australia.

Space telescopes

One of the difficulties that astronomers with Earth-based telescopes have to deal with is the presence of Earth's atmosphere. The atmosphere distorts pictures, which is why many telescopes are located high up in the mountains, where the atmosphere is thinner. Also, the atmosphere blocks some kinds of radiation from objects in space. The only way astronomers can study these objects is to use telescopes above our atmosphere – in space.

It wasn't possible to do this before the development of rockets and vehicles like the space shuttle. Now, space telescopes are a reality.

Telescopes in orbit

Space telescopes are instruments in space that are used to observe planets, stars, galaxies, and other objects. Many were launched into orbit by the space shuttle, including the Hubble Space Telescope.

The Hubble Space Telescope has been sending back brilliant images from space for more than 20 years.

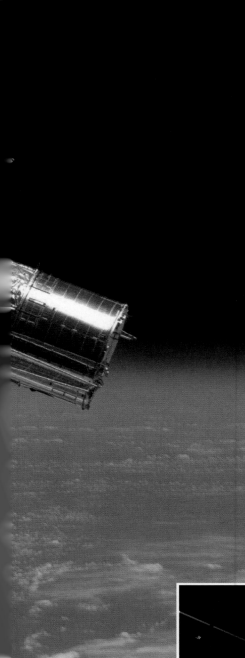

Hubble

On April 24, 1990, the space shuttle and crew of mission STS-31 were launched to put the Hubble Space Telescope into low Earth orbit. It was one of the most powerful science instruments ever developed and began a new era in astronomy. After 20 years of service, it has taken around half a million photographs of objects in space.

Gamma rays

Some space telescopes are built to collect and measure high-energy gamma rays. This can't be done using surface telescopes as gamma rays are absorbed by our atmosphere. Gamma rays can come from pulsars, black holes, supernovas and neutron stars.

The Fermi Gamma-ray Space telescope studies pulsars and high-energy sources of gamma rays.

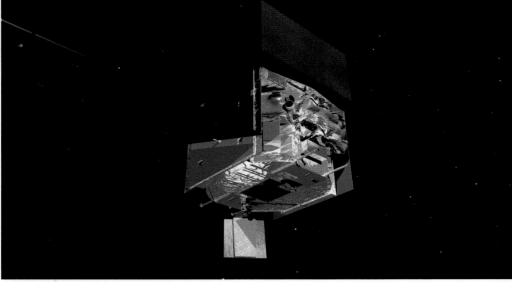

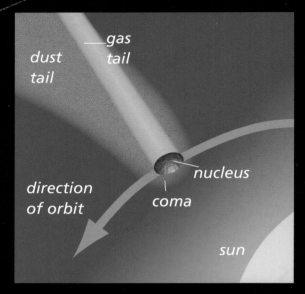

A comet's bluish gassy tail always points away from the sun. The separate dust tail is slightly curved.

This is the comet known as Hale-Bopp, photographed as it passed through the constellation of Andromeda.

COMETS

Well beyond the planets of our solar system lies a cloud of material left over from the solar system's birth – the Oort cloud. It's made up of lumps of ice and dust ranging in size from tiny splinters to large chunks hundreds of miles across. Most of them remain in the same orbit around the sun. But every so often one breaks away and moves towards the inner solar system – probably affected by the gravity of a nearby star. It's called a comet.

Comet tails

As the comet nears the sun it speeds up. Its outer layers of ice are warmed up and turn directly to gas. The gas forms a haze called a coma around the main part, or nucleus, of the comet. When the comet gets inside the orbit of Jupiter the haze is affected by the solar wind. The haze is blown into a long, bluish tail that always points away from the sun. Any dust that was frozen in the nucleus is also blown away, but in a separate tail that is yellow and slightly curved.

Elliptical orbits

Comets move around the sun in an elliptical orbit (like a flattened circle, or oval). Some comets swing around the sun and back out into deep space, taking thousands of years to return. Others may become trapped in smaller orbits by the gravity of the planets, especially that of Jupiter. They return more often.

VACATION IN SPACE

When we think of space travel we think of astronauts carrying out experiments or servicing satellites and space stations. But some people will travel into space for a vacation – as tourists.

The first paying passenger to travel into space was a billionaire businessman from California who vacationed for eight days aboard the International Space Station (ISS). Seven more tourists followed, each traveling to the ISS aboard a Russian Soyuz spacecraft. The price of the flights was around $20–35 million. There are now plans to offer trips on a spacecraft that will orbit the moon. There are also plans to build a space hotel to orbit Earth.

The VSS Enterprise is the spacecraft that Virgin Galactic will use to take passengers into space.

Inside the cabin, passengers will experience weightlessness.

Virgin Galactic

Virgin Galactic has built the first manned commercial spacecraft. So far more than 300 people have signed up to venture into space with Virgin. These will be suborbital flights that will offer around six minutes of weightlessness and the sight of the curved Earth.

LUNAR LANDING

The moon is the closest body in space to our Earth. So it made sense to send a mission to land human beings on the moon rather than any of the solar system's planets.

Apollo

NASA's Apollo project was designed to land the first humans on the Moon — and to get there ahead of America's space rivals, the USSR. There were 17 Apollo missions. The first six were unmanned test flights. The rest were manned space flights, which included the first moon landing, in 1969.

Saturn rockets were used to launch the Apollo spacecraft. They were three-stage assemblies that had the Apollo module perched on top.

Men on the Moon

It all began in 1961 when President John F. Kennedy declared that he wanted to land humans on the moon by the end of the decade. NASA knew they were ready for the task and after test flights and manned flights around the moon, Apollo 11 was prepared for the first moon landing.

With Neil Armstrong, Edwin "Buzz" Aldrin, and Michael Collins on board, the great *Saturn 5* rocket lifted off on July 16, 1969. Four days later the Lunar Module descended to the moon's

surface and Armstrong and Aldrin became the first men to walk on the moon. Collins stayed aboard, where he did experiments and took photographs. The two astronauts spent three hours on the moon collecting rocks and performing more experiments. On July 24 they returned safely to Earth.

Future landings

Future landings on the moon are planned, when astronauts will search for resources that might be of value on Earth. They'll also learn how to work in a difficult environment, which will prepare them for further space travel. Scientists will carry out experiments to investigate how the planets were formed, as the moon offers clues to what actually happened.

Neil Armstrong steps on to the moon's surface.

HELPING HAND

Become an astronomer

One way to learn more about space firsthand is to become an amateur astronomer. All you'll need is a small telescope or a good pair of binoculars – and a very dark sky – and you can begin. The positions of the stars and planets change with the seasons: you can find maps of the night sky online or in books about star-watching. The moon is a good place to start.

Keep up with NASA

You can learn a lot more about space and space exploration by visiting the NASA Education Web site and clicking on your age group. The more you learn about our universe, the better prepared you'll be to look after it. There's plenty to read and watch as well as fun games to play.

Watch for satellites

Satellites from NASA's Jet Propulsion Laboratory and other sources monitor the planet, including its oceans and atmosphere. NASA publishes details of how you can track several of these satellites, and find them when they might be visible in the night sky where you live. The International Space Station (ISS) is also visible to the human eye as it orbits Earth, for just a few minutes at a time at any one location.

Learn the sky

Learn the main constellations so that you can find your way around the night sky. Spot Polaris, the pole star, so

that you always know where north is. Grab a pair of binoculars and look at the craters on the moon, or track a comet. At certain times of year, meteor showers occur — find out when these are in your area and watch the shooting stars.

Museums

Many cities have superb museums devoted to space and astronomy. Try to visit one of these and see a lump of meteorite, a real spacecraft, or even some dust from the moon for yourself. A planetarium is a special dome-shaped theater that shows you exactly what you see when you look up at the night sky.

Astronaut for a day

Explore the ISS on the NASA Web site, find out what the current crew are up to and how they live, and play an interactive game that challenges you to fix real problems that have occurred on real space missions.

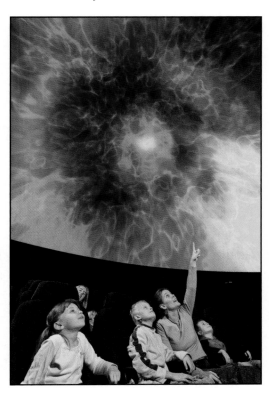

Space in school!

Some schools every year can link, via NASA, with the ISS, ask the crew questions and watch them performing experiments. These events are streamed on the Internet, so if your school is not so lucky, you can still watch them happening.

GLOSSARY

alpha particle The nucleus of an atom of helium.

asteroid A medium-sized rocky object orbiting the sun.

astronaut A man or woman who has been trained to fly in space. Known as a cosmonaut in Russia.

astronomer A scientist who studies the stars.

astronomy The study of the stars.

atmosphere A blanket of gases that surrounds a planet, a moon or a star.

Aurora Borealis Bands of colored lights that appear in the night sky in the northern hemisphere. Similar lights in the southern hemisphere are called Aurora Australis.

Big Bang The theory that all the matter and radiation in the universe started at one moment in time about 15 billion years ago.

carbon dioxide A colorless, odorless gas.

Ceres The largest asteroid in the solar system.

CFC (chlorofluorocarbon) A gas that used to be used in refrigerators and aerosol cans (now banned in most countries). A major cause of the hole in the ozone layer.

coma A thin cloud of gas and dust surrounding the nucleus of a comet.

comet A frozen mass that travels around the sun in an elliptical orbit.

corona The outer part of the sun's atmosphere.

crater A circular hollow made by the impact of a meteorite or formed by the rim of a volcano.

debris The dust, rock, and metal remains of things that have broken up in space.

eclipse What happens when the light from one body is blocked by another. A solar eclipse occurs when the moon passes between the sun and Earth.

electromagnetic radiation Radiation such as light, radio waves and X rays made up of electric and magnetic waves that travel at the speed of light.

electron A particle with a negative charge.

elliptical Oval-shaped (as in elliptical orbit).

equator An imaginary line around the widest part of Earth (or other body), dividing it into the northern and southern hemispheres.

galaxy A very large group of stars held together by gravitational pull.

gamma ray Very high frequency electromagnetic radiation.

gravity The force of attraction that pulls objects towards Earth's core.

Hale-Bopp A very bright comet last visible from the Earth in 1995–1997.

helium A very light, colorless inert gas.

Hubble Space Telescope An orbiting observatory launched by the United States in 1990.

hydrogen A colorless, odorless, highly flammable gas that is the lightest and most abundant element in the universe.

ISS (International Space Station) An international research facility that is being assembled in a low orbit around Earth.

light (wave) A form of radiation that is visible to the human eye.

magnetic field The field of force produced by a magnetic object, which is evident from the effects it produces on other magnetic objects.

Mars One of the planets in the solar system.

meteor A small piece of solid material from outer space that hits Earth's atmosphere, usually burning up when it does so.

meteorite A piece of solid material from outer space that is large enough to reach Earth without burning up.

microbe A microscopic organism, a minute life form.

moon A natural satellite of any planet.

NASA National Aeronautics and Space Administration – the American government agency responsible for the US space program.

neutron star The dense remains of a massive star, left behind after a supernova explosion.

Northern Lights see Aurora Borealis.

nucleus The center part of a comet, composed of ice and rock.

Oort cloud A huge collection of comets and debris orbiting the sun in the outermost regions of the solar system.

optical telescope An astronomical telescope that uses mirrors to reflect an image to the observer.

orbit The path taken by one object around another in space. Very often elliptical.

oxygen A colorless, odorless, tasteless and nonflammable gas that makes up 21 percent of the volume of the air we breathe.

ozone A form of oxygen that can absorb ultraviolet radiation in the upper atmosphere.

Pallas A large asteroid in our solar system, discovered in 1802.

penumbra A partially shaded area around the edges of the shadow in an eclipse.

photon A particle of electromagnetic radiation.

photosphere The luminous visual surface of a star, such as the sun.

planet A celestial body that orbits a star.

polar orbit An orbit that passes over the North and South poles.

proton A particle with a positive electric charge.

Proton rocket A Russian rocket used for the launch sector of space exploration.

pulsar A small, spinning neutron star that sends out electromagnetic radiation.

radiation Energy that is radiated or transmitted in the form of rays or waves or particles.

radio telescope An astronomical telescope that picks up radio waves from space.

radio wave A kind of electromagnetic radiation.

rocket A missile or other vehicle that moves by squirting out a jet of fluid or gas from a rocket engine.

satellite A natural or artificial (man-made) body in an orbit around another body, such as the sun or a planet.

shooting star The visible path of a meteor as it burns up when it enters Earth's atmosphere.

singularity The tiny point from which the universe started according to the Big Bang theory.

solar flare A burst of energy on the surface of the sun.

solar sail A sail designed to catch the energy of the sun's light and use it to power a spacecraft.

solar system The sun and all the celestial bodies in its orbit, including the planets and their moons, asteroids, and everything else.

solar wind A stream of gas, protons and electrons that flow from the sun at speeds of up to 217 miles (350 km) per second.

Soyuz (spacecraft) A series of spacecraft designed for the Soviet space program.

space junk All the leftover debris from past space programs.

space probe An unmanned spacecraft launched to explore various planets, moons, asteroids and comets of the solar system.

space shuttle A spacecraft that is capable of landing back on Earth and being used several times.

space telescope A telescope launched into outer space and used to observe distant planets, stars, and galaxies.

Sputnik 1 The world's first artificial satellite, launched by the USSR on October 4, 1957.

star A hot, glowing, gaseous celestial body, visible at night from Earth as a point of light.

sun The star in the center of the solar system, which provides light and heat for the planets.

sunspot An area of the sun's surface that is cooler than the surrounding area and that usually appears black on photographs.

supernova An exploding star.

telescope A scientific apparatus for viewing distant objects.

ultraviolet (UV) rays A type of electromagnetic radiation with very short wavelengths, which is normally blocked or filtered by the ozone layer.

umbra The darkest part of the shadow during an eclipse; also the dark center of a sunspot.

universe The totality of everything that exists, considered as a whole – from our solar system to other stars and galaxies to intergalactic space.

Venus One of the planets in the solar system.

weightlessness Having little or no weight because of being free from the effects of gravity.

INDEX

aerosol 21

alpha particle 17

Andromeda 36

Apollo 40

Arecibo 32

asteroid 7, 26, 28, 29,

astronaut 11, 12, 13, 17, 21, 38, 41

astronomer 4, 19, 22, 28, 34, 42

astronomy 35

atmosphere 8, 15, 17, 20, 21, 24, 26, 27, 31, 34, 35, 42

Aurora Borealis 17

Big Bang 4

black hole 35

carbon dioxide 30, 31

Ceres 28

CFC (chlorofluorocarbon) 20, 21

Columbia 11

coma 36, 37

comet 26, 27, 36, 37, 43

corona 19

crater 27, 29, 43

CubeSail 15

debris 14, 15, 26

eclipse 18, 19

Edwin "Buzz" Aldrin 40, 41

electron 17

equator 6

European Space Agency 14

galactic cosmic ray (GCR) 21

galaxy 4

gamma ray 17, 21, 35

gas 4, 16, 17, 20, 22, 36, 37

geosynchronous 6

gravity 6, 9, 22, 24, 28, 37

Hale-Bopp 36

helium 16

Hubble Space Telescope 11, 34, 35

hydrogen 16

immune system 20

ISS (International Space Station) 11, 12, 38, 42, 43

Jupiter 6, 7, 28, 29, 37

light wave 22

lunar landing 40

magnetic field 6, 16, 17, 22, 23

magnetic pole 22

Mars 28, 30, 31

meteor 26, 27, 43

Michael Collins 40

microbes 30

micrometeorite 26

micrometeoroids 25

mirror 24, 32

moon 9, 18, 19, 38, 40, 41, 42, 43

moon rocks 41

moon walk 41

NASA 11, 40, 42, 43

Neil Armstrong 40, 41

neutron star 22, 23, 35

northern lights 17

Oort cloud 37

Opportunity 30

optical telescopes 32

orbit 4, 6, 7, 8, 9, 10, 11, 12, 14, 15, 18, 26, 27, 28, 29, 30, 34, 35, 36, 37, 38, 39

oxygen 20, 21
ozone 20, 21
Pallas 28
particle 16, 17, 26
Pathfinder 30
penumbra 18, 19
photon 24
photosphere 16, 17
planet 4, 6, 7, 9, 26, 28, 29, 30, 31, 41, 42
planetarium 43
polar orbit 6
proton 17
Proton rocket 12
pulsar 22, 35
radiation 17, 20, 21, 22, 34
radio telescope 32, 33
radio wave 17, 22, 32, 33
rocket 6, 10, 11, 12, 14, 15, 24, 34, 40
rover 30, 31
satellite 6, 8, 9, 11, 14, 15, 32, 38, 42
shooting star 26
Siberia 14
singularity 4
solar array 12
solar energy 20, 30
solar flare 16, 17
solar prominences 16
solar sail 24, 25
solar system 4, 7, 28, 37, 40,
solar wind 17, 21, 37
Soyuz spacecraft 38
spacecraft 14, 24, 28, 30, 38, 39, 40, 43
space junk 14, 15
space probe 6, 30

space shuttle 10, 11, 12, 15, 34
space station 11, 12, 38
space telescope 6, 11, 34, 35
space walk 17
Spirit 30
Sputnik 8
star 4, 16, 22, 23, 34, 37, 42, 43
sulphuric acid 30
sun 4, 7, 16, 17, 18, 19, 20, 21, 22, 26, 27, 30, 36, 37
sunspot 16, 17
supernova 21, 22, 35
telescope 6, 10, 11, 19, 32, 33, 34, 35, 42
trojan 29
ultraviolet (UV) rays 20
umbra 18, 19
universe 4, 8, 42
US Space Surveillance Network 14
Venus 7, 30
Vesta 28
Viking 30
Virgin Galactic 39
VSS Enterprise 39
weightlessness 39
X ray 17
Zarya 12

PHOTO CREDITS

(t=top, b=bottom, l=left, r=right, m=middle)

Pg 1 – NASA
Pg 2/3 – NASA
Pg 5 – NASA
Pg 6/7 – NASA
Pg 7 – (b) NASA
Pg 8 – (b) NASA
Pg8/9 – NASA
Pg 9 – (t) NASA, (m) NASA, (b) NASA
Pg 10/11 – (b) NASA, (t) NASA
Pg 12/13 – NASA
Pg 13 ¬– (t) NASA, (b) NASA
Pg 15 – (t) NASA
Pg 14/15 – (b) NASA
Pg 16/17 – NASA
Pg 17 – Jostein Hauge / Shutterstock
Pg 18/19 – (b) Larry Landolfi / Science Photo Library, (t) Rev.
Ronald Royer / Science Photo Library
Pg 19 – Dmitry Kosterev / Shutterstock
Pg 20/21 – (b) NASA
Pg 21 – Aida Ricciardiello / Shutterstock
Pg 23 – NASA
Pg 24/25 – NASA
Pg 25 – Bettmann / Corbis
Pg 26/27 – Dr Fred Espenak / Science Photo Library
Pg 27 – Walter G Arce / Shutterstock
Pg 28 – NASA
Pg 29 – (t) NASA, (b) NASA
Pg 30 – NASA
Pg 31 – NASA, (insert) NASA
Pg 32 – Eckhard Slawik / Science Photo Library
Pg 32/33 – (t) Dr Seth Shostak / Science Photo Library, (b)
Ilya Genkin / Shutterstock
Pg 34/35 – NASA
Pg 35 – NASA
Pg 36/37 – NASA
Pg 38/39 – NASA
Pg 39 – NASA
Pg 40 – NASA
Pg 41 – NASA
Pg 42/43 – (tl) Picture Contact / Alamy
Pg 43 – (t) Archimage / Alamy, (b) NASA